I0016013

Agile Alchemy: Transforming Chaos into **Success** with **Scrum**

By David Dragan

Foreword

This book is part of an experimental series, in which the author seeks to explore the power of generative language models, in particular OpenAI's Generative Pre-trained Transformer 3 (GPT-3) within a solely utilitarian approach to writing educational materials.

For far too long books presenting themselves with an educational façade have been long-windedly circumventing direct, relevant, and *helpful* discourse.

The author sincerely believes there is a case to be made for the utility (and dare one say, indispensability) of generative language models in the writing of scholastic resources.

Special thanks are extended to the team at OpenAI for their humanitarian ethos in opening their GPT-3 model for use by the general public, and their continued efforts to ensure safety and accuracy.

1 TABLE OF CONTENTS

Table of Contents 4

1Introduction to Agile Scrum 8

1.1Understanding Agile Methodologies.................. 10

1.2Origins and Evolution of Scrum 10

1.3Principles of Agile Manifesto.............................. 11

1.4Key Concepts of Scrum Framework..................... 12

1.5Chapter Summary.. 12

2Foundations of Scrum... 13

2.1Scrum Roles and Responsibilities 13

2.1.1Product Owner: 13

2.1.2Scrum Master: 13

2.1.3Development Team: 14

2.2Scrum Events 14

2.2.1Sprint: 15

2.2.2Sprint Planning: 15

2.2.3Daily Scrum:.. 15

2.2.4Sprint Review:... 16

2.2.5Sprint Retrospective: 16

2.3Artifacts in Scrum 16

   2.3.1Product Backlog:... 17

   2.3.2Sprint Backlog:.. 17

   2.3.3Increment: 17

   2.3.4Definition of Done: 18

2.4Chapter Summary... 18

3Implementing Scrum 19

3.1Getting Started with Scrum 19

3.2Forming Agile Teams 19

3.3Setting Up Product Backlog 20

3.4Sprint Planning and Execution............................. 20

3.5Daily Scrum Best Practices................................... 21

3.6Conducting Effective Sprint Reviews.................... 22

3.7Sprint Retrospective Techniques......................... 22

3.8Scaling Scrum for Large Projects 23

3.9Scrum in Different Contexts 23

3.10Chapter Summary.. 24

4Advanced Scrum Practices... 25

4.1Refinement of Product Backlog........................... 25

4.2Advanced Sprint Planning................................... 26

4.3Continuous Integration & Delivery...................... 26

4.4Agile Testing Strategies 27

4.5Agile Estimation and Planning Poker.................. 27

4.6Agile Metrics and Reporting 28

4.7Handling Dependencies in Scrum........................ 28

4.8Agile Leadership and Coaching............................ 29

4.9Chapter Summary.. 29

5Evolving with Scrum 30

5.1Agile Transformation Journey 30

5.2Overcoming Common Challenges 31

5.3Sustaining Agile Culture....................................... 31

5.4Agile Maturity Models.. 32

5.5Future Trends in Agile and Scrum 32

5.6Chapter Summary... 33

6Appendices 34

6.1Glossary of Agile and Scrum Terms..................... 34

6.2Recommended Reading and Resources 36

7Final Words... 37

Agile Alchemy

Transforming Chaos into Success with Scrum

Agile Alchemy

"Every effort has been made to condense the material presented in this book to a succinct yet exhaustive few chapters. I sincerely hope that through this short read you are able to extract maximal value and gain a comprehensive understanding of the facts presented."

1 INTRODUCTION TO AGILE SCRUM

1.1 UNDERSTANDING AGILE METHODOLOGIES

Agile methodologies represent a paradigm shift in project management and software development practices, emphasising flexibility, collaboration, and iterative development over traditional sequential approaches. Rooted in the need to adapt to rapidly changing business environments and customer requirements, Agile methodologies prioritise delivering value incrementally and continuously, thereby fostering customer satisfaction and stakeholder engagement.

1.2 ORIGINS AND EVOLUTION OF SCRUM

Scrum, one of the most widely adopted Agile frameworks, traces its origins back to the early 1990s when it was introduced by Jeff Sutherland and Ken Schwaber. Initially conceived as a means to improve software development processes, Scrum has since evolved into a versatile framework, applicable across various industries and domains. Drawing inspiration from empirical process control theory and lean principles, Scrum advocates for self-organizing, cross-functional teams working in short, time-boxed iterations called sprints to deliver shippable increments of work.

1.3 PRINCIPLES OF AGILE MANIFESTO

The Agile Manifesto, a seminal document drafted in 2001 by a group of software developers seeking better ways of building software, encapsulates the core values and principles behind Agile methodologies. At its heart, the Agile Manifesto prioritises individuals and interactions over processes and tools, working software over comprehensive documentation, customer collaboration over contract negotiation, and responding to change over following a plan. These principles emphasise adaptability, customer-centricity, and continuous improvement as fundamental tenets of Agile approaches.

1.4   KEY CONCEPTS OF SCRUM FRAMEWORK

Central to the Scrum framework are several key concepts that shape its structure and practices. These include defined roles such as the Product Owner – responsible for maximising the value of the product, the Scrum Master – tasked with facilitating the Scrum process, and the Development Team – accountable for delivering the product increment.

Additionally, Scrum prescribes specific events, including Sprint Planning, Daily Scrum, Sprint Review, and Sprint Retrospective, to enable transparent communication, inspection, and adaptation throughout the development cycle. Moreover, Scrum employs artifacts such as the Product Backlog, Sprint Backlog, and Increment to facilitate shared understanding, alignment, and progress tracking within the team and stakeholders.

1.5   CHAPTER SUMMARY

In summary, an understanding of Agile methodologies, particularly the origins and evolution of Scrum, along with the principles of the Agile Manifesto and key concepts of the Scrum framework, provides a solid foundation for leveraging Agile practices effectively in project management and software development endeavours.

2 FOUNDATIONS OF SCRUM

Scrum, a prominent Agile framework, is built upon a solid foundation comprising distinct roles, events, and artifacts. Understanding these foundational elements is crucial for effective implementation and successful adoption of Scrum practices within organisations.

2.1 SCRUM ROLES AND RESPONSIBILITIES

The Scrum framework defines three primary roles, each with specific responsibilities aimed at driving collaboration, transparency, and accountability throughout the development process.

2.1.1 Product Owner:

The Product Owner serves as the primary stakeholder representative, responsible for maximising the value delivered by the product. This entails defining and prioritising the items in the Product Backlog, ensuring alignment with business goals, and communicating the product vision to the development team. The Product Owner acts as the single point of accountability for product decisions and is actively engaged in providing feedback and guidance to the team.

2.1.2 Scrum Master:

The Scrum Master is a servant-leader who facilitates the Scrum process and ensures adherence to its principles and practices. This role involves removing impediments, fostering a culture of continuous improvement, and coaching the team to enhance their effectiveness and self-organisation. The Scrum Master acts as a shield for the team, protecting them from external distractions, and facilitates collaboration between the team and stakeholders.

2.1.3   Development Team:

The Development Team consists of professionals with the skills necessary to deliver the product increment. This self-organising, cross-functional team collaborates closely to transform the items from the Product Backlog into a potentially shippable increment during each sprint. The Development Team is accountable for delivering high-quality work, maintaining a sustainable pace, and continuously improving their processes and practices.

2.2   SCRUM EVENTS

Scrum events, also known as ceremonies, provide structured opportunities for the Scrum Team to inspect and adapt their work. These events enable transparency, inspection, and adaptation, fostering a culture of empirical process control and continuous improvement.

2.2.1   Sprint:

A Sprint is a time-boxed iteration, typically lasting two to four weeks, during which the Scrum Team works to deliver a potentially releasable increment of the product. Sprints provide a predictable cadence for development and serve as a framework for managing risks and complexity.

2.2.2   Sprint Planning:

Sprint Planning is a collaborative event where the Scrum Team determines the work to be performed during the upcoming Sprint. The Product Owner presents the prioritised items from the Product Backlog, and the Development Team selects the items they believe they can complete within the Sprint. The outcome of Sprint Planning is a Sprint Goal and a Sprint Backlog, detailing the work to be undertaken.

2.2.3   Daily Scrum:

The Daily Scrum, also known as the daily stand-up, is a short (typically no more than 15 minutes), time-boxed meeting held every day of the Sprint. It provides an opportunity for the Development Team to synchronise their activities, inspect progress towards the Sprint Goal, and identify any impediments requiring resolution. The Daily Scrum is conducted by the Development Team and facilitated by the Scrum Master.

2.2.4   Sprint Review:

The Sprint Review is a collaborative event held at the end of the Sprint to review the increment and gather feedback from stakeholders. The Development Team demonstrates the work completed during the Sprint, and stakeholders provide input that may influence the Product Backlog. The Sprint Review serves as an opportunity to validate assumptions, gather insights, and adapt the Product Backlog as needed.

2.2.5   Sprint Retrospective:

The Sprint Retrospective is a structured meeting held at the end of each Sprint to reflect on the team's processes and identify opportunities for improvement. Each member of the Scrum Team inspects how they worked together during the Sprint and collaboratively devise strategies for enhancing their effectiveness and efficiency in subsequent Sprints. The Sprint Retrospective encourages a culture of continuous learning and adaptation within the team.

2.3   ARTIFACTS IN SCRUM

Scrum artifacts are tangible outputs that provide transparency and insight into the work being performed and the progress made towards achieving the Sprint Goal.

2.3.1   Product Backlog:

The Product Backlog is an ordered list of all the features, enhancements, and fixes required for the product. It serves as the sole source of truth for all the work that needs to be done, with items prioritised based on their value and dependencies. The Product Backlog is owned and managed by the Product Owner, who continuously refines and adjusts it based on feedback and changing priorities.

2.3.2   Sprint Backlog:

The Sprint Backlog is a subset of items from the Product Backlog selected for implementation during the current Sprint. It represents the work committed to by the Development Team and serves as a plan for achieving the Sprint Goal. The Sprint Backlog is dynamic and may evolve throughout the Sprint as new information emerges or priorities shift.

2.3.3   Increment:

The Increment is the sum of all the completed and potentially releasable Product Backlog items developed during a Sprint. It represents the tangible outcome of the team's effort and serves as a measure of progress towards achieving the project's goals. Each increment should be of high quality, meeting the Definition of Done and ready for review by stakeholders.

2.3.4   Definition of Done:

The Definition of Done is a shared understanding within the Scrum Team of what it means for a product backlog item to be considered complete. It encompasses all the criteria, including quality standards, testing requirements, and acceptance criteria, necessary for an item to be potentially shippable. The Definition of Done ensures transparency and consistency in the team's work and serves as a guideline for achieving high-quality deliverables.

2.4   CHAPTER SUMMARY

In summary, the foundations of Scrum are built upon defined roles and responsibilities, structured events, and tangible artifacts that enable teams to collaborate effectively, deliver value iteratively, and adapt to changing requirements. Mastery of these foundational elements is essential for harnessing the full potential of Scrum and realising the benefits of Agile principles in one's project management and software development endeavours.

3 IMPLEMENTING SCRUM

Implementing Scrum within an organisation requires careful planning, execution, and ongoing refinement to ensure its successful adoption and integration into existing processes. This chapter delves into various aspects of implementing Scrum, including forming Agile teams, establishing essential rituals, and scaling Scrum for large-scale projects and diverse contexts.

3.1 GETTING STARTED WITH SCRUM

Embarking on the journey of adopting Scrum begins with understanding its principles and practices and fostering a culture of agility within the organisation. It involves educating stakeholders about the benefits of Agile methodologies and garnering buy-in from leadership to support the transition. Establishing clear objectives and success criteria, as well as identifying champions and advocates within the organisation, can significantly contribute to a smooth adoption process.

3.2 FORMING AGILE TEAMS

Forming Agile teams involves assembling cross-functional, self-organising groups capable of delivering value iteratively. It requires identifying individuals with diverse skill sets and fostering a collaborative mindset focused on achieving common goals. Creating stable, dedicated teams and providing adequate training and support are essential for enabling team members to effectively collaborate and perform their roles within the Scrum framework.

3.3 SETTING UP PRODUCT BACKLOG

The Product Backlog serves as the backbone of Scrum, containing a prioritised list of features, enhancements, and fixes required for the product. Setting up the Product Backlog involves collaborating with stakeholders to capture and refine requirements, prioritise backlog items based on value and dependencies, and continuously groom the backlog to ensure it remains relevant and actionable. Establishing clear acceptance criteria and ensuring alignment with the product vision are crucial for maximising the value delivered by the Scrum team.

3.4 SPRINT PLANNING AND EXECUTION

Sprint Planning marks the beginning of each Sprint, during which the Scrum Team collaboratively selects and commits to delivering a set of backlog items. It involves defining a Sprint Goal, identifying the tasks necessary to achieve the goal, and estimating the effort required for each task. Effective Sprint Planning requires active participation from the Product Owner, Scrum Master, and Development Team, as well as a clear understanding of the team's capacity and capabilities.

Sprint Execution involves the Development Team working iteratively to deliver the committed backlog items. It requires a focus on collaboration, transparency, and adaptability, with daily stand-up meetings (Daily Scrum) providing an opportunity for the team to synchronise their efforts, identify obstacles, and adjust their plan as needed. The Scrum Master plays a crucial role in removing impediments and facilitating the team's progress, while the Product Owner remains engaged to provide guidance and clarify requirements throughout the Sprint.

3.5 Daily Scrum Best Practices

The Daily Scrum, or daily stand-up meeting, serves as a cornerstone of Scrum, providing a forum for the Development Team to inspect progress and adapt their plan daily. Best practices for conducting Daily Scrums include keeping the meeting time-boxed and focused, standing up to encourage active participation and brevity, and emphasising collaboration and problem-solving. Encouraging open communication, culturing a positive team atmosphere, and addressing impediments promptly are essential for maximising the effectiveness of Daily Scrums.

3.6 Conducting Effective Sprint Reviews

The Sprint Review is a collaborative event held at the end of each Sprint to review the increment and gather feedback from stakeholders. Conducting effective Sprint Reviews involves showcasing the work completed during the Sprint, soliciting input from stakeholders, and validating assumptions against the product vision. It requires active engagement from the Product Owner and Development Team, as well as a focus on gathering actionable feedback to inform future iterations.

3.7 Sprint Retrospective Techniques

The Sprint Retrospective provides an opportunity for the Scrum Team to reflect on their processes and identify opportunities for improvement. Employing various retrospective techniques, such as Start - Stop - Continue, Liked - Learned - Lacked - Longed For, or Sailboat Retrospective, can help facilitate meaningful discussions and uncover insights to enhance team collaboration and performance. Encouraging open and honest communication, fostering a blame-free environment, and prioritising actionable outcomes are key to conducting effective Sprint Retrospectives.

3.8   SCALING SCRUM FOR LARGE PROJECTS

Scaling Scrum for large-scale projects involves adapting the framework to accommodate increased complexity, multiple teams, and distributed environments. Approaches such as Scrum of Scrums, Nexus, LeSS (Large-Scale Scrum), or SAFe (Scaled Agile Framework) offer guidance and practices for scaling Scrum effectively. Establishing clear communication channels, aligning goals and dependencies across teams, and fostering a culture of collaboration and knowledge sharing are critical for successfully scaling Scrum in large projects.

3.9   SCRUM IN DIFFERENT CONTEXTS

Scrum's applicability extends beyond software development to various domains, including marketing, HR, and beyond. Adapting Scrum to different contexts requires understanding the unique challenges and demands of each domain and tailoring the framework accordingly. Whether applying Scrum to manage marketing campaigns, streamline HR processes, or enhance organisational agility, the principles of transparency, inspection, and adaptation remain fundamental for achieving success.

3.10 CHAPTER SUMMARY

In summary, implementing Scrum requires a concerted effort to establish a supportive environment, form cohesive teams, and adopt Agile practices effectively. By embracing the principles of Scrum and adapting its practices to suit diverse contexts, organisations can unlock the potential for innovation, collaboration, and continuous improvement in their projects and processes.

4 ADVANCED SCRUM PRACTICES

As organisations mature in their adoption of Scrum, they often seek to explore and implement advanced practices to further enhance the effectiveness and efficiency of their Agile processes. This chapter delves into a range of advanced Scrum practices, offering insights into refinement techniques, planning strategies, technical practices, and leadership approaches aimed at maximising the value delivered by Scrum teams.

4.1 REFINEMENT OF PRODUCT BACKLOG

The refinement of the Product Backlog is a continuous activity aimed at ensuring that backlog items are well-defined, appropriately prioritised, and ready for implementation. Advanced refinement techniques involve collaborative sessions with stakeholders and the Scrum Team to elaborate on backlog items, clarify requirements, and identify dependencies. These sessions may include story mapping, value stream mapping, or impact mapping to facilitate shared understanding and alignment among team members. By investing time and effort in refining the Product Backlog, organisations can minimise uncertainty and maximise the efficiency of Sprint execution.

4.2 ADVANCED SPRINT PLANNING

Advanced Sprint Planning techniques focus on enhancing the effectiveness and efficiency of the Sprint Planning process, ensuring that the Scrum Team is well-prepared to commit to delivering a valuable increment of work. Techniques such as timeboxing, capacity-based planning, and risk-based planning help teams prioritise and select backlog items based on their complexity, dependencies, and potential impact. Moreover, the use of story points, velocity tracking, and historical data analysis can aid in more accurate estimation and forecasting, enabling teams to set realistic Sprint goals and commitments.

4.3 CONTINUOUS INTEGRATION & DELIVERY

Continuous Integration and Delivery (CI/CD) practices are integral to achieving agility and responsiveness in software development. Advanced Scrum teams leverage automation, version control, and build pipelines to integrate and deliver code frequently and reliably. By adopting CI/CD practices, teams can reduce integration overhead, minimise the risk of defects, and accelerate the delivery of value to customers. Moreover, incorporating automated testing, code reviews, and deployment pipelines into the development workflow promotes collaboration, transparency, and quality assurance throughout the development lifecycle.

4.4 AGILE TESTING STRATEGIES

Agile testing strategies focus on embedding testing activities seamlessly into the development process, enabling teams to detect and address defects early and often. Advanced testing practices include test-driven development (TDD), behaviour-driven development (BDD), and exploratory testing, which emphasise the importance of testing as a collaborative and iterative process. By involving testers, developers, and other stakeholders in test design and execution, teams can ensure that software meets quality standards, user requirements, and acceptance criteria from the outset.

4.5 AGILE ESTIMATION AND PLANNING POKER

Agile Estimation and Planning Poker are techniques used by Scrum teams to estimate the effort and complexity of backlog items collaboratively. Advanced estimation practices involve using relative sizing, reference stories, and expert judgment to refine estimates and improve accuracy over time. Planning Poker sessions encourage team members to share their perspectives, leverage their collective knowledge, and reach a consensus on the size and priority of backlog items. By accepting uncertainty and embracing a mindset of continuous improvement, teams can refine their estimation practices and enhance their ability to deliver value predictably.

4.6 AGILE METRICS AND REPORTING

Agile Metrics and Reporting provide valuable insights into team performance, progress, and value delivery, enabling organisations to make informed decisions and drive continuous improvement. Advanced Agile metrics go beyond traditional measures of productivity and focus on outcomes, such as customer satisfaction, cycle time, and business impact. By tracking and analysing metrics such as lead time, throughput, and defect rates, teams can identify bottlenecks, mitigate risks, and optimise their processes for maximum efficiency and effectiveness.

4.7 HANDLING DEPENDENCIES IN SCRUM

Handling dependencies effectively is essential for ensuring that Scrum teams can deliver value consistently and predictably. Advanced techniques for handling dependencies involve identifying, prioritising, and mitigating dependencies early in the development process. This may include establishing cross-team coordination mechanisms, implementing interface agreements, or restructuring the product backlog to minimise interdependencies. By proactively managing dependencies, teams can reduce delays, improve alignment, and maintain a sustainable pace of delivery.

4.8 AGILE LEADERSHIP AND COACHING

Agile Leadership and Coaching are critical for fostering a culture of collaboration, innovation, and continuous improvement within Scrum teams. Advanced leadership practices involve empowering teams, fostering trust, and promoting servant leadership principles. Agile coaches play a vital role in supporting teams, facilitating ceremonies, and removing impediments to progress. By providing guidance, mentorship, and feedback, Agile leaders and coaches enable teams to overcome challenges, embrace change, and achieve their full potential.

4.9 CHAPTER SUMMARY

In summary, advanced Scrum practices encompass a range of techniques and approaches aimed at optimising team performance, enhancing product quality, and maximising value delivery. By embracing refinement techniques, planning strategies, technical practices, and leadership approaches, organisations can unlock the full potential of Scrum and realise the benefits of Agile principles in their projects and processes.

5 EVOLVING WITH SCRUM

The evolution of Scrum within organisations encompasses a dynamic journey of transformation, adaptation, and continuous improvement. This chapter delves into various aspects of evolving with Scrum, including navigating the Agile transformation journey, overcoming common challenges, sustaining Agile culture, exploring Agile maturity models, and anticipating future trends in Agile and Scrum methodologies.

5.1 AGILE TRANSFORMATION JOURNEY

The Agile transformation journey represents a fundamental shift in organisational mindset, culture, and practices towards embracing Agile principles and values. It involves aligning business objectives with Agile practices, advocating collaboration and transparency across teams, and empowering individuals to embrace change and innovation. The Agile transformation journey typically unfolds in iterative stages, involving pilot projects, training and education initiatives, and organisational restructuring to support Agile ways of working. Successful Agile transformations require strong leadership commitment, stakeholder engagement, and a willingness to experiment, adapt, and learn from failures.

5.2 OVERCOMING COMMON CHALLENGES

The path to Agile maturity is fraught with challenges and obstacles that organisations must overcome to realise the full benefits of Agile methodologies. Common challenges include resistance to change, lack of alignment between business and IT, organisational silos, and cultural inertia. Overcoming these challenges requires a holistic approach, involving clear communication, stakeholder engagement, and a focus on building trust, transparency, and collaboration. By addressing root causes, encouraging a culture of continuous improvement, and providing support and resources, organisations can navigate challenges effectively and sustain their Agile journey over the long term.

5.3 SUSTAINING AGILE CULTURE

Sustaining an Agile culture is essential for embedding Agile principles and practices into the fabric of the organisation. It involves cultivating a mindset of openness, experimentation, and continuous learning, where individuals are empowered to take ownership, collaborate across functional boundaries, and embrace uncertainty and change. Sustaining an Agile culture requires ongoing reinforcement of Agile values, rituals, and behaviours through leadership support, coaching and mentoring, and recognition of achievements and contributions. By creating an environment where experimentation is encouraged, failure is viewed as an opportunity for learning, and diversity of thought is celebrated, organisations can sustain their Agile culture and thrive in an increasingly complex and competitive landscape.

5.4   AGILE MATURITY MODELS

Agile maturity models provide a framework for assessing an organisation's readiness and maturity in adopting Agile practices and principles. These models typically define a set of criteria, benchmarks, and maturity levels that organisations can use to evaluate their Agile capabilities and identify areas for improvement. Examples of Agile maturity models include the Agile Maturity Model (AMM), Agile Capability Assessment (ACA), and SAFe Agile Maturity Assessment (AMA). By benchmarking their performance against industry standards and best practices, organisations can gauge their progress, prioritise initiatives, and drive continuous improvement in their Agile journey.

5.5   FUTURE TRENDS IN AGILE AND SCRUM

The future of Agile and Scrum is shaped by emerging trends and developments in technology, business, and market dynamics. Future trends in Agile and Scrum include the convergence of Agile with DevOps and Lean principles, the rise of Agile at scale frameworks, such as

SAFe, LeSS, and Nexus, and the integration of Agile practices into non-IT domains, such as marketing, HR, and finance. Additionally, advancements in technology, such as artificial intelligence, machine learning, and cloud computing, are likely to influence the way Agile teams collaborate, innovate, and deliver value in the future. By staying abreast of emerging trends, experimenting with new approaches, and developing adaptability and resilience, organisations can position themselves for success in an increasingly Agile world.

5.6 CHAPTER SUMMARY

In summary, evolving with Scrum involves navigating the Agile transformation journey, overcoming common challenges, sustaining Agile culture, exploring Agile maturity models, and anticipating future trends in Agile and Scrum methodologies. By embracing change, collaboration, and building a mindset of continuous improvement, organisations can evolve with Scrum and realise the full potential of Agile principles and practices in driving business agility and innovation.

6 APPENDICES

6.1 GLOSSARY OF AGILE AND SCRUM TERMS

Agile: A set of values and principles for iterative and incremental development, emphasising flexibility, collaboration, and customer satisfaction.

Scrum: An Agile framework for managing complex projects, characterised by short iterations called sprints and a focus on delivering value incrementally.

Product Owner: The individual responsible for maximising the value of the product and managing the Product Backlog.

Scrum Master: The servant-leader responsible for facilitating the Scrum process and removing impediments to the team's progress.

Development Team: A cross-functional group of professionals responsible for delivering the product increment.

Sprint: A time-boxed iteration in Scrum, typically lasting two to four weeks, during which a potentially releasable increment of work is completed.

Sprint Planning: A collaborative event at the beginning of each Sprint where the Scrum Team plans the work to be done and commits to a Sprint Goal.

Daily Scrum: A short, time-boxed meeting held every day of the Sprint for the Development Team to synchronise their activities and plan the day's work.

Sprint Review: A collaborative event at the end of each Sprint where the Scrum Team demonstrates the completed work to stakeholders and gathers feedback.

Sprint Retrospective: A meeting at the end of each Sprint where the Scrum Team reflects on their process and identifies opportunities for improvement.

Product Backlog: An ordered list of all the work that needs to be done on the product, maintained by the Product Owner.

Sprint Backlog: A subset of items from the Product Backlog selected for implementation during the current Sprint.

Increment: The sum of all the completed and potentially releasable product backlog items developed during a Sprint.

Definition of Done: A shared understanding within the Scrum Team of what it means for a product backlog item to be considered complete.

6.2 RECOMMENDED READING AND RESOURCES

"Scrum: The Art of Doing Twice the Work in Half the Time" by Jeff Sutherland

"Agile Estimating and Planning" by Mike Cohn

"User Stories Applied: For Agile Software Development" by Mike Cohn

"The Lean Startup: How Today's Entrepreneurs Use Continuous Innovation to Create Radically Successful Businesses" by Eric Ries

"Agile Retrospectives: Making Good Teams Great" by Esther Derby and Diana Larsen

7 FINAL WORDS

This book is the first of the experimental series and has proved to have been a fascinating and deeply rewarding endeavour.

As mentioned in the Foreword at the beginning of this short book, OpenAI's GPT-3 language model has been utilised for the purpose of text generation. I first asked the model to outline an appropriate structure for a short book serving as a comprehensive introduction to Agile Scrum. Subsequently, I tasked it with writing each chapter according to the structure it had defined, upon which I compiled all of its outputs, proofread, researched to ensure verity of the facts promulgated, edited in places for enhanced clarity and readability, and added the "human touches" such as the typography, visual hierarchy, and graphics.

Such an undertaking would have certainly required just shy of a month's work to research and author manually, therefore I hope you too can see the sheer potential of AI's utilisation within the context here presented.

I would like to conclude by thanking you for taking the time to read this short book, and hope you close it armed with new-found knowledge that will serve you faithfully in your future Agile with Scrum endeavours.